WILD

WILD

BEN OKRI

LONDON · SYDNEY · AUCKLAND · JOHANNESBURG

1 3 5 7 9 10 8 6 4 2

First published in 2012 by Rider, an imprint of Ebury Publishing

Ebury Publishing is a Random House Group company

Copyright © 2012 Ben Okri

Ben Okri has asserted his right to be identified as the author of this work
in accordance with the Copyright, Designs and Patents Act 1988.

The Random House Group Limited Reg. No. 954009

Addresses for companies within the Random House Group
can be found at
www.randomhouse.co.uk

A CIP catalogue record for this book is available from the British Library

The Random House Group Limited supports The Forest Stewardship
Council (FSC), the leading international forest certification organisation.
All our titles that are printed on Greenpeace approved FSC certified
paper carry the FSC logo. Our paper procurement policy can be found at
www.randomhouse.co.uk/environment

Printed and bound by CPI Group (UK) Ltd, Croydon, CR0 4YY

ISBN 9781846043307

Copies are available at special rates for bulk orders. Contact the sales
development team on 020 7840 8487 for more information.

To buy books by your favourite authors and register for offers, visit
www.randomhouse.co.uk

'One thunderbolt strikes root through everything.'

Heraclitus

Material in this collection has previously appeared as follows:

'As Clouds Do Drift' (2010), 'I Sing a New Freedom' (2009 – one of the world's first twitter poems) and 'New Year Poem: O that Abstract Garden' (2011) on twitter and www.riderbooks.co.uk; 'Dark Light' on Granta.com (2011); 'Heraclitus' Golden River' in *Ode* magazine (2007); 'Lines *in Potentis*' commissioned for the London Assembly (Dec 2002); 'Migrations' commissioned by the Barbican Centre (1999) & published in *Tin House* 49 (2011); verses from 'More Fishes than Stars' set to music by Harper Simon on *Harper Simon* (Universal Music, 2009) and verses from 'The Core' on iTunes; 'On Klee' in *Birds of Heaven* (Orion, 1995); 'On the Oblique in Horace' in *The Horatian* magazine (1998); 'Solidified Volcanic Lava, Olduvai Gorge' in *Daily Telegraph* (2011); 'The Blue Cloth (Mozambique)' on *Work in Progress*, BBC Radio 3; 'The Golden House of Sand' as 'Children of the Dream' in *Guardian* (21 Aug 2003); 'The Ruin and the Forest' in *London* magazine (July 2002); and 'The Soul of Nations' in *Guardian* (20 Jan 1999).

CONTENTS

MY MOTHER SLEEPS

My mother is sleeping
On my battered armchair.
It is night, and I have
Become a child again.

I remember her in my childhood years
Sleeping in dark corners
Where the rats chew the garri sacks
In our hot little room,
Or on wooden chairs in the green
Darkness, or on cement platforms
Near the gutter of the unforgiving
Street, through the unhappy nights
And the suffering years.
The remembrance rouses
In me dreams of strength,
And dreams of fear.

I watch over her as she gently sleeps.
The soft dreams flutter her eyelids.
Her quiet breathing, and the blessedness
Of kindly eyes that are shut tight
And the parted lips soothe
My anxious soul.
She is travel-weary
And has found her son.

How patiently she stayed awake
All those years, watching over us
In our heaving worrisome sleep
Of childhood, watching our
Future become our past.

Now that she sleeps
In my battered armchair
I know that she dreams well.
I am watching over her.
My turn has come round at last.

BEGIN WITH A LEAP

For Beezy Bailey and Brian Eno

Someone said begin with a leap.
And so I leapt over the great
Sleep, with a heavy stone
In my head. But I was light
As a song, or an African
Bird, one you might
See in the safari of dreams.
So when I leapt over,
Where did I land?
These are questions for the sand.

It turns out the great sleep
Is a giant wall that's made
Of inverted flowers,
Or songs that are sung
Inside out, if you know
What I mean.

When they wring you dry,
With pain and life and death,
When they break your legs
With blades and with feathers,
When they squeeze the mystery
Out of you, all that's left
Is that stone, heavy as the earth.

Then they ask you to leap
Over your own death,
Without much hope;
And how do you do that,
In the sea or on land
Without drowning, without
Singing your protest in a sound?
These are questions for the sand.

But my hour drew near.
All the things I made
Were full of fear.
The flames and the birds
Were all that I could hear.
And as the night came on,
With pollen settling on the glass
Ceiling, and darkness grew
From all the lonely songs
In millions of lonely places,
And as the wings of death
Surrounded this ledge where
We stood before the great abyss,
That's when someone
Said, 'Begin with a leap.'

And like a lioness,
Like a piercing trumpet
Note, like the first colour of dawn,
Or like the brilliant tail-feathers
Of a love-struck peacock, or even
Like a shy kiss that starts a fire,
A touch that makes
A generation, or like rain
That covers the dry fields
With the music of the oracle,
I leapt right over the great sleep,
With a magnet in my heart.

MORE FISHES THAN STARS

For Harper Simon

1.

Everyone seems so certain.
And everyone knows who they are.
Everyone's got a mother and a father.
Everyone knows where they're going,
And seems so sure they're going far.
Everyone's got more friends than they can use,
(And they don't see how too much can confuse)
Except me, because I'm a Fool.
I'm simple as a bee.
But it doesn't matter,
There are more fishes than stars.
There are more fishes.

2.

Everyone seems so sure of themselves.
And everyone is brimming with success.
Everyone seems to know money
Will bring them the real happiness.
Everyone's just been on holiday in the sun,
Or are just coming back from one.
They seem to have so much fun.
Everyone's with the latest thing,
(They don't seem to feel life's hidden sting)
Except me, because I'm a Fool.
I don't use everyone like a tool.
I'm simple as a melody in C.
But it doesn't matter,
There are more wishes than stars.
There are more wishes.

3.

I'm not too certain about many things.
And I'm not too sure who I am.
I ain't got no mother and no father.
I'm slow, like the trees when they grow.
I'm sluggish, like the ocean when it moves.
And I love all things with a secret glow.
I'm plain, like water or like rain.
And I think it's unlucky to complain.
I'm easy, like a fish that's free.
Or like that melody in C.
But it doesn't matter,
There are more fishes than stars.
There are more fishes.

4.

I'm not chasing success.
I'd like to transcend happiness.
And I'm not sure if money is the meaning of life,
Or whether it conquers all strife.
I ain't been on holiday for some time,
And I don't think that's such a crime.
I sit still, like an oak tree on a hill.
Open to the all, like a window in a wall.
But it doesn't matter,
Because I get to go to the source (of the sea)
Where the mother of all things looks after me.
There are more fishes than stars,
More wishes than stars.

FROM THE CHRONICLES

For Brian Eno

1.

When I was a boy
The birds came from
The underworld.
They flew out from our dreams,
From all across Albion.
They rose from the sweet
Songs of the dead,
From the chronicles
Of Vikings and Saxons
Wedded to earth and sea.

Sometimes the birds
Made noises like old fuzz-boxes,
And we loved the distortion
Of things, of sounds, faces.
The guitar of ancient voices.

The birds were all lovers.
There were women that sang
In rich colours.
Ox-blood is for their passion.
When the flowers are blissful –
The colour of deafness –
The birds sound quaintly like
Millions of pins dropping,
Or like drum-riffs of rain.

15

2.

I remember my father's funeral,
And I remember the sound
Of people howling with laughter.
The laughter wasn't about
Him; but with the slightest
Joke anyone made the birds
Rose from our laughter, soared –
And the women were aglow.
We had been released.

When I was a boy
The birds came from
The underworld.
They came from the sunrise.

And now there are standing
Stones where the underworld
Used to be, and jars of honey.
And streets of solemn women.

DREAMING BY THE WATER OF LEITH

For Susie Nicklin

I wish that I could sleep
Again the way a child
Does at an art show, deep
And with its little drooping head
Sunk in a fluid world
Where all things are more real:
A wizard who changes stones
Into clouds, or a mouse
Who talks and sings lovely
Melodies from the blue window
Of the red and gold house
Where the rainbows are made.
And on the rainbows angels prayed.

I watch the child's grandfather take
The sleeping child around
The gallery in a pram. They make
A tour of pictures about stones
And symbols in vast natural landscapes.
Walking art, walking dreams.
The child sleeps deep in a better
World, while I dreamily linger
In time, weaving with insomnia.

Like the mellifluous voice of an opera singer,
The ale-coloured river rolls over slate.
The lush hair of the water-plant streams
In the current. I float past the tranquil
Drama of waterfalls, thinking
About the artist's ambivalent fate,
And wishing I could sleep again
Like a child does, and still create.

17

A LOVE SONG

When on another day
You see me smile
Know that I have emptied
My silver cup
In quiet lamentation
Of your absence.

Your peacock-coloured shawl
Brings the joy of secret
Times to my solitude.

I sing when your nude form
And joyful face of blue
Makes the night stray
Into my sea-chambers.

I hide my wounds
In the intoxication
Of your dark remote eyes.

The mingled laughter in bars
Draws the bow of my ecstasy:
Out of my bleeding love
I pluck the fiery arrows.

I loved you in five cities
And love you still in dim places
Where mirrors have replaced
The laughter of risen angels.

THE SIGN

To inscribe the pentagram
While speaking the magic
Upon which the power of man
Rests, transforms the tragic,

And makes of it the gold of Time.
The star of Merlin, or the seal
Of Solomon: all symbols rhyme
With the dreams of the real.

Belief should rest on what we know.
What we know rests
On what we sow.
Truth will endure all tests.

So speak the star
And the circle that contains all.
Symbols come from afar.
We shan't fall further than our fall.

A WEDDING PRAYER

For Ieva and Ivor

There's gold in the sky today.
Saturn's hand is loosened.
And Venus with her rose
And myrtle glows in the horizon.
There's a special conjunction
In the air. Love has brought two
Rivers into one way, one dream;
Has sown the quilt of harmony.
And scattered some magic
Fragrance upon the sea.

Love inspires many metaphors;
But marriage inspires
A single prayer that encompasses
The future and many undreamt
Generations. It's not that two
Souls become one. It's that
Two souls realise a common soul,
A shared goal, mutual journey
Into one another's hearts.

That's what I mean. Travel
Into one another, as into
A country you have long admired,
And read many fables about,
And now find yourself
Before its famed rivers,
Its inspiring mountains.

Exchange hearts, and become
A little bit more the other;
Shape together a magic life
Of dreams, of ideals, and wisdom.
In love stories they talk too much
About love, but not enough of wisdom,
Of commonsense like salt
Or dew much loved of alchemists.
Marriage is more than strong passions
Or a home of too many emotions.
It is a house of royal reason, good
Sense, kindness and, above all,
Friendship. If for a poet I sound
Prosaic, then you miss my beat.

Be the greatest friend to one another.
Isn't that what we always dreamt
About as children, and have spent
All our lives seeking, in so many missed
Connections? The ancients say that
We seek our missing soul.
I say we seek our missing destiny
In the loving best friend we seek
For all our days. The one
Who never judges us,
But always raises us.

This is what I wish for you two:
That you live the fairytale
Which eludes many, made
Of the faithful strings of the violin,
The solid wood of the piano,
And the intelligence that
Turns every night into a song,
Every day into a garden,
Every quarrel into a fine harvest
Of understanding. May
Your journey together be
The adventure that life
Was always meant to be;
May you never lose your
Laughter, your playfulness,
And your music. Be the wise
Children of the earth.
Be fruitful in enchanting deeds
And in futures. Be something
Rare in this much misunderstood
Tale of life: may your love
Help you find that hidden
Gold in the unfinished hours,
That your life together, long
In years, rich in stories,
May yield the tranquillity of flowers.

VIRGIL IN BRINDISI

He drifted into harbour
Lying in state
When the wine-drenched
Sea was clean as a slate.

He dreamt of his great poem
Restless within him unfinished;
And he wept that twelve years
Beyond death were needed
For its perfection to remain undiminished.

The great emperor, vertical,
On another galley, was on a practical
Mission, in a changing imperial sky.
He could never have guessed
That in his poet's unrest
An eternal world would soar high.

TALISMAN FOR THE JOURNEY

We are walking amongst monsters.
Some of us have spells
Against the birdman.
Some of us, love devours.
Some of us are looking
At the constellations.
These flowers are protection
Against evil.

We are all nailed to the cross
Of the economy.
Mannequins have taken over
The high street.
On the whole we love
What is unreal.

But we are saved
From the monsters
By the birds.
We walk among monsters
Because we're outsiders.
We are all born into
The labyrinth.

Follow the song
Or the birds or the colours
Or the voice unheard.
Follow the unseen thread
Past the weeping woman
And the white flowering tree
And those who have died alive
Without a song in their heads,
Past the half-men half-beasts
Who were once boys who loved
Women, but now are minotaurs
Devouring beauty and the dawns.

Follow the unheard song
Past the totems
Past eyes that see horrors
And cannot speak,
Past the grim artisans
Of the king.
Go past them all
With the magic of the one thing,
That flower of multiple bloom,
With which to charm
The monsters and the dead.

LINES *IN POTENTIS*

One of the magic centres of the world;
One of the world's dreaming places.
Ought to point the way to the world:
For here lives the great music of humanity,
The harmonisation of different
Histories, cultures, geniuses, and dreams.
Ought to shine to the world and tell
Everyone that history, though unjust,
Can yield wiser outcomes.
And out of bloodiness can come love;
And out of slave-trading
Can come a dance of souls;
Out of division, unity;
Out of chaos, fiestas.

City of tradition, conquests and variety;
City of commerce and the famous river,
Tell everyone that the future
Is yet unmade.
Many possibilities live in your cellars:
Nightmare and illumination,
Boredom and brilliance.
Tomorrow's music sleeps
In undiscovered orchestras,
In unmade violins,
In coiled strings. Spring waits
By the lakes, listening
To the unfurling daffodils.
Summer lingers with the hyperborean worms,
Awaiting an astonishing command
From the all-seeing eye of Ra.

Tomorrow's music sleeps
In our fingers, in our awakening
Souls, the blossom of our spirit,
The suggestive buds of our hearts.

Tell everyone the idea
Is to function
Together, as good musicians
Would, in undefined future orchestras.
Let the energy of commerce
Flow. Let the vision of art heal.
Technology, provide the tools.
Workers of the world,
Re-make the world
Under the guidance of inspiration
And of wise laws.
Create the beautiful
Music our innermost
Happiness suggests. Delight the future.
Create happy outcomes.

And while Autumn dallies
With the West wind
And the weeping nightingales,
And Winter clears its sonorous throat
At the Antipodean banquets, preparing
For a speech of hoarfrost
And icicles conjured from living breath,
I want you to tell everyone
Through trumpets played
With the fragrance of roses, that
A mysterious reason has brought us
All together,
Here, now, under the all-seeing
Eye of the sun.

THE SOUL OF NATIONS

The soul of nations do not change;
They merely stretch their hidden range.
Just as rivers do not sleep,
The mind of empire still runs deep.

Into a river many waters flow
The merging and conquest – history's glow.
A gathering of native and alien streams,
Of turbulent and tranquil dreams.

Classes overflow their rigid boundaries
Slowly stirring dreary quandaries:
Accents diverse ring from its soul,
A richer music revealing the whole.

New waves from abroad shake the shores,
Disturbing the sleep of the resonant bores.
But the gods of the nation do not change.
Their ways are deep and often strange.

History moves, and the surface quivers,
But the gods are steadfast in the depth of rivers.

THE SCREAMER

Three days after the massacre
In Jenin, with the bulldozed dead
Under the rubble and men shot
Down and children blinded
By the blast of tanks
That crushed their frail houses
Into powder and blood,
And a man in a hot room
Howling for two white days
With no-one to help him,
And with the town blocked off
So that the massacre
Could be unleashed without
Any foreign witnesses,
Entering legend by rumours
And grief only; three days
Afterwards, when the air
Of the world was poisoned
With silence and complicity,
The superpowers stood
By and watched with eyes
Averted from the future
Catastrophe that would be born
From the unforgetting rage.

Three days on, when I thought
The world no longer fit
To live in, when strange prophecies
That had nibbled my pen
Had become birds of doom
In the Spring, I went out
For a walk to find some
Sanity among boats that do not
Travel out to the sea,

Along the silver road
Of the canal.
Then as I crossed the blue
Bridge, a golden red sun
Fading over the church,
The air was stunned
By the sudden eruption
Of that which words
Dare not describe.
The screams burst on the air,
And three men stood frozen
On their boat, and knew
The horror of a hell not seen,
In the gasping shock of their stance.
Three times the scream
Shook the trees, the waters,
And the clouds, shook the bridge,
The houses, and the frozen hearts
That no longer remember
What feeling is meant for.
Three times the scream sounded,
Like one in a nightmare
Imprisoned, or like one possessed
By an evil spirit that won't
Depart reasonably,
Won't be exorcised,
Or one whom madness had
Taken over, or upon whose body
A tank slowly rode across
With plenty of time to die
In agony, the screams intended
To remind us what pain
Really meant, in case . . .

And then I saw the cracked figure
In a red coat, saw her
Like a crazed opera singer
Shake and pause for deep breath
Before descending infernal
Depths to release again
The chaos of the scream's
Source, the volcanic heart
Of the city, the world,
As it staggers towards insanity.

She would scream, in long bursts,
Then walk on suddenly
As if she were normal
Again; and when all had
Returned to their activities,
Grateful no-one was being
Murdered, she'd scream some more,
As if unknown to us she was
Screaming out all of our
Unscreamed screams
From the seabed of our neuroses,
Neck deep in the abyss,
Under the fading sun.
Further along I passed a girl
With earplugs on;
She'd heard nothing.
A man staggered out of a pub,
And hitched up his trousers.
A lovely young lady wandered
Towards me and I asked
If I had imagined the red woman
Screaming. 'No, often she does this,
By day and by night,' I was told.

'For two months now, she has been
At it. Not violent at all.
But she seems angry afterwards.
Can't seem to control it.
First time I witnessed her,
It shook me so. Now I'm
Reconciled. She's ill, I suspect,
And mostly does it along the canal.
So long as she screams, I guess,
She'll be alright. Getting it out,
I think, does her a world of good.
I'd love to do it too,
If I could. Maybe she screams
For us all, don't you think?'

Down the canal path I went
And thought and didn't think.
Walked out my screams.
On the way back I remembered
How I howled when told on the phone
That my mother had died.
If I had screamed
Much longer than I had
I would have gone quite mad.
If I hadn't screamed at all
My heart would have stopped,
And my eyes gone dark, and cold.
I saw the screamer through
The iron railings and the weeds.
She strode in red,
And all about her
The world – our world – bled.

MINING DIAMONDS

Metal in the eyes of lovers
Wreaks fear
On the possibility of music.
The fear awakens

Calvary on the face of stone,
Flowers that breed on rock
And magnify the sorcery
Of infiring anger.

Sweet waters that rankle
Beneath the bridgehead spread
Rust shimmering with revolt
In the dark deadly season.

The hills tremble.
Stones unlock their waters;
Waves of fire spread
Over visions of serenity.

We feel so little, and deny
So much. Whose are those hands
Milking poison with touch, whose eyes
In their metallic gaze?

Bitter dreams track
Violence with much hunger:
The murders beneath the wreckage.
The smell of blossom on fingers

Dissolves the metal in my soul.
My stone is overturned.
But steel shadows
Keel about me.

I like the invented prophet
Who said: 'I walk true on rivers
Of the mind. On the face of savagery,
I mine diamonds.'

THE WORLD IS RICH

They tell me that the world
Is rich with terror.
I say the world is rich
With love unfound.
It's inside us and all around.

Terror is there, no doubt:
Violence, hunger and drought;
Rivers that no longer
Flow to the sea.
It's the shadow of humanity.

There's terror in the air.
And we have put it there.
We have made God into an enemy,
Have made God into a weapon,
A poverty, a blindness, an army.

But the world is rich with
Great love unfound:
Even in the terror
There is love, twisted round
And round. Set it free.

River, flow to the sea.

THE BLUE CLOTH

(Mozambique)

She unwound the blue cloth
To the amazed cameras.
Her nine children stood around her
As clear an evidence
Of life as joy itself.
Against the flood, under
Which houses were submerged,
And trees were drowned,
And half the country had become
The bed of a wild river,
Against all this disaster,
And so many dead,
The blue cloth seemed insufficient
A reply to the doubting mind.

It had been the end of time
Seen in advance. When the flood
Came families lost everything.
The world had watched as people fled
To safety on rooftops,
And treetops; and witnessed
A woman giving birth among
The inhospitable branches.
Against all this, the blue
Cotton cloth seemed inadequate.

And the mother, face radiant
With a faith lost to the memory
Of our age, told how she thought
Herself abandoned by Him who
Had promised eternal friendship
To all humanity as she found
Herself high up in the tree.

But with the long blue cloth,
She wove an embroidery of safety,
In and out of the arms
Of her nine children,
And saved them all in the great
Tree when all else had failed.
The best things often seem
Insubstantial in times
Of real crisis.

A simple cloth is more
Powerful than the mighty nations
Who look on, and do nothing.
Love is a blue cloth in a flood.

THE GOLDEN HOUSE OF SAND

After Martin Luther King

1.

They won't be satisfied
Till they've had more,
The children of the dream
Who know what real dreaming is for.
Their hunger won't be denied.
For they are draped
In all the colours of the sun;
And they sing and grow from
Pain's conviction.
They will not be satisfied
Their love for life will
Not be denied
Till they have had much more.

2.

But what more do they want?
O, they want the earth and the stars,
To break out of all bars,
And they want the beautiful heavens too.
Just so you know,
That they want to be free,
Free as the sea,
And want the possibilities
That freedom brings
And the note that it rings:
That bright music of flight,
Its unsuspected height.

They also want freedom's
Weight, and its deep dark side.
They know you cannot hide
From the Kingdom's
Yin and its yang,
From life's duality.

3.

They do not want to be defined.
They don't want to be limited.
And they want their fire refined.
And they want to love who they want,
And for it not to be such an affront.
They do not want to beg
For their humanity,
Or for the right to be
Creative, different, or surprising,
Or wild, or defying
Of boundaries.
They do not want condescension,
Or imprisoning assumptions.
They want the freedom to rebel,
Even against themselves.
They want sometimes to ring
A new unruly bell, without going to hell.
They want to celebrate,
Even that which didn't celebrate them.
They want to taste the fruits
Of the earth, in music, art, science
And dreams. They want to calibrate
The depth and height of man's spirit.
They want to be the best
That freedom promises,
Without explanations,
Without apologies.

hey want to astonish,
Casually, like the angels do.
And they want to amaze,
Simply, the way geniuses can.
They want the right to fail,
Bravely, like great explorers will.
They want to quest, nobly,
Like passionate pilgrims
On the red roads of time.
Nothing should be too big
Or too quirky for them to dream
And to accomplish
In this golden house of sand.

5.

They are more than they seem.
And no prison of mind or steel
Can hold them down any more.
We who are children of the dream
Know what real dreaming is for.

We are bursting open the dark door.

SOLIDIFIED VOLCANIC LAVA, OLDUVAI GORGE 1.2 MILLION YEARS AGO

For Neil MacGregor

We break the rock;
The force within it screams.
Now we have the power to make.
Who knows what the rock knows?
We do. We know the fire inside.

Ancestors from the sky
Broke through the broken form.
We have the power.

Time, food and animals
Wake up now as we crack
From the father this shape.
It's like the skull of war.
Weapon of blood to make
Fire, to make hunger die.

We have broken the night.
The night yields in the rock.
Night leaps out from our hands.
The night has left the sky
As fire and power in our hands.
As a strong shape.
The world is ours at last.

41

We are as the gods dream.
Haven't we broken the mountain
And shaped the world
In our own hands, to bend and crack
And change it into form and dream?

We have become more than we seem.

THE FORGOTTEN ODYSSEUS

Odysseus never finds the same woman
He left behind. He lost her in the songs
Of the bird-like sirens, under the belly
Of the sheep, in the one-eyed sleep
Of Polyphemus, and the dreams of Calypso.

When he finds her again, woven into
The hallucinations of his dangerous
Homecoming, the old dog, as much travelled
In dreams as its master, remembers when
Time was new, without the war love started.

Penelope, veiled and hiding from lusting
Suitors, remembers a man less old, less
Wily, less haunted by the endless seas,
The alien suns and pullulating wars:

A man unknown for whom Ithaca is not
Homecoming, but the first broken journey
Towards a forgotten way of dying.

THE RUIN AND THE FOREST

1.

Their order has become our chaos.
Their order is a chaos to us –
We cannot find our way through it.
They created their order
Out of the chaos they found:
This became a standard.
But they never intended
To create a standard for us,
To fix a way, a road:
They shaped in relation
To the chaos that they found.

We have to create order
Out of the chaos we find.
And the order of the ancients
Is part of our chaos too.
We can't find a clear way through it.
What was clear and straight to them
Is not so clear and straight to us.
We are winding, twisted.
We need winding and twisting ways
For us to travel straight.

2.

You can develop habits of mediocrity
Just by doing what is required.
Creation should be new every time:

New in relation to the chaos that is there.
Chaos is new all the time.
It is renewed every night.
Creation must be re-born
With the new light
With the new dawn.
New every day.

But yesterday's standard is becoming
A part of today's chaos.
A strange alien language.
Needing footnotes, explanations.
A rich forest of misunderstandings.
Start again the new road at dawn.
Yesterday's road has led
To yesterday's destination.
Today is a new chaos.
A new journey. A new city.
Needing new paths. And new standards.

3.

Habit is thus a great
Force of nature.
When used blindly,
Without wisdom,
In the creation of art
It cultivates a fruitful mediocrity.
Hitched to a great new dream
Or vision it is a mighty
Secret for the creation of marvels
And enduring pyramids of creativity.

So long as you start with your chaos.
Order from the chaos that you find.
The chaos of now, today;
Of which the order and standards
And classics of the past are a part.
The way a ruin is part of a forest,
Part of its mystery, its beauty,
Its dereliction, its reversion,
To untrammelled wildness.
Civilisation returning home to nature.
Form returning to the mother.
Begin again.

4.

The new plays against the old.
The old is disappearing into the abyss
From which we hear faint and poignant
Songs of supernal harmony –
Songs of the original spirit,
The original, the shaping dream,
Shaping against the chaos
A human yearning and love,
The eternal need for harmony
Against a chaos conquered and lost.

5.

Those songs are guides.
Our song should resonate
The primal one.
But singing anew from our breast
Against the greater chaos
In which all that was great
In the past was a part.
A greater chaos
For having greater orders in it too.
O, how to be so true,
Here, now, among the mighty ruins
That we no longer understand.
And the forest that's all around,
And the darkness that we have found,
The need to feel our way,
Find our way, in the dark,
Over the flood, to our ark,
Across the legends that hide their blood,
And give the now a resonant shape
And music that moves the walls to form
And the birds to listen,
To move nature with our mastery,
And win for humanity
A clear way through the labyrinth
Of our flowing mortality,
Towards the secret harmony
Of the stars and the sun
And the absolute Hum.

PIANO

For Daisy Leitch

Out of the shining wood
Out of the quiet light
Of its sounding
A blue bird emerges
Soars and touches
The sickle moon that rides
A crescent cloud
In the darkness of a blue sky;
And then a tender music fills
The dream of an Italian evening
In the hall where a child
Dances alone
Before the sea of light.

Out of the bright mirror
A clear world stands
Waiting. Do we
Dare to enter,
Or follow the strange call
To a new shore
Where Time is more?
Where to dream is to love
And to love is to give?

There are no spaces
But are full of unheard
Melodies, colours of spirit.
Arches mirror
The curved universe within,
As the sky mirrors our
Secret eternity.

Out of the drawing she
Sits as on moonbeams of delight.
All things are made
Of a divine music, you know.
When we're happy
Doesn't it show?
We glow
As if the primal word
Plays so in us,
Shining
Through our transparent flesh,
The god in us singing
To the god about us.

THE RHINO

My horn stands me apart
And I have a passionate heart.
My skin is a thick crust.
I walk in the wonder of dust.

WILD

There's a surprise at the end.
Everything should connect
With everything. The brain
Cools the blood, and the blood
Cools thought. Those ancients saw
The world as it is,
A system of co-operation,
Where things are both themselves
And symbols and correspondences.

Might it not be that a movement
Of paint here on plain wood
Is a retreat on a distant
Battlefield; or that a child
Moving counters on a blue
Tarpaulin is an upward curve
In the moment of a sleeping civilisation?

The strumming of a guitar moves
A faraway village to its harvest.
A child cutting cane-brakes
In a fading farm might cut
The knot that opens a new time
Of peace in the mysteries
Of the Middle East.
A snail crushed on a road
Could be the birth
Of a nation state.
A dog barking in the East
Might free the economies in
The sultry South.
A lover's breathing in the depth
Of a Winter's night
Could be a moment's cool
Inspiration in the southern seas.
A dreamer tossing coins
In an underwater city could
Have launched the thought
That led to relativity.

The reality of the sun
In the music of the earth.

A dolphin falls in love,
And there are a million
Pregnancies in the minds of men.
A salmon's leap
Is a philosopher's insight.
Cosmologies are born
When statues dance.
A poet's thought
Unfurls unknown constellations.
The movement of the brush,
The ovulation of colours,
Sends dreams through the Milky way.
Reconciliation of friends
Is music to the ghosts.
And a thought of love
Sends the hint of the tuberose
To the smiling afterlife.

But how much of over there,
Like the tug of a universal web
Falls like hail or change here?
Some of our best moments
Are the reverse thoughts
Of our dead mothers.

And that wild inspiration
Which surprises thinkers,
And poets, inventors and musicians
In the ambivalent dawn,
The inspiration after fatiguing
Work, after despair, after every line
Has been exhausted;
The flash that turns the world
Upside down and therefore
The right way up at last,
Was it not the backward
Flowing world blood from Elysium,
Where masters of the unknown
Pipe lovely melodies
Through the fountains
And the gardens,
Through the infinite dialogue
Of the big and small,
Seen and unseen,
Felt and unfelt,
Like lovers coming back
From death?

DARK LIGHT

On a night when my soul was damp
I found in the street a dark lamp.
The moon was cold and green,
The sky had a sinister sheen.

I lit the lamp and stumbled about.
I'd not gone far when I heard a shout.
And then I saw a nasty sprite
Emerging from the lamp's bleak light.

'It's not every night that I'm brought awake,
And now I'm going to make the world shake.'
This nasty sprite led me on
To a dark place beyond the sun,
Where evil ghouls and tyrants played
And danced in that infernal shade.

As long as that strange lamp was lit
There was no hope for me.
And in that darkness there were only
Nasty things to see.

And all because my soul was damp
And lit the light of a dark lamp.

TOWARDS THE SUBLIME

Have you noticed that in all true
Transformations what emerges
Is stranger than before,
And higher, richer, magical?

It is as if mass yields
Light, or pure power, pure
Vision given upward
Form beyond form –
Transcending all the laws
Of its previous condition.

And so chrysalis into butterfly,
Water into wine, death
Into life, weight into
Flight, burden into illumination,
Enchantment into the freedom
Divine:

Out of all that was there before,
This bright new thing.
A living testament
To the sublime within,
Given new being.
Beyond measure.
A joy to the ages.

CLOUDS

So there are times
When one necessarily mines
The hidden wisdom of the heart
Within the mountains of the mind
And finds therein the undiscerned
Beauty of the clouds and mankind.

So there are times
When one has no magical rhymes
For those moods of the sea
That come vaguely over me.
And I seek in the sky
A consolation from on high.
But then a melody of light
Transforms the night.

THE CORE

I looked so much I could not see
And in everything I looked at only saw me.
The sky isn't really blue you know
Leaves of grass are not really green.
I want to drink in all the beauty in the world.
Especially the things not seen.

Many of the stars I see are not really there.
Waves of light move in a way not entirely clear.
I watch the birds till I stop thinking about flight.
I gaze at the river till I am lost in light.

What was I afraid of, always hiding my eyes?
I've got to face my truth, and my lies.
I have got to stop wanting to be in control.
Being at peace is a much better goal.

(I'm just learning what eyes are for.
To see with the heart, see right to the core.)

TO THE FULL MOON

For Keith Magnay

You return, dream-transformer,
With the roundness of the world.
You bring celestial mysteries
In your tailwind.
The earth quivers under your glow;
And the core of man, fertile
And amorphous like the core of sleep,
Responds to the tidal sweep
Of your sun-charged stone.
Like a celestial bowl of milk,
You nourish our secret
Selves with that invisible food
Of the heavens. Every living thing
Is enchanted by that silent
Song you sing. Stones
Grow under your power.
Forests enlarge their terrestrial
Dream. Waters swell and rise
Up to you, climbing the hidden
Stairs of your magnetic light.
Women grow strong and strange
With your visions as with the children
Of a star-touched womb.
We curve towards you, and become
Elliptical under your spell.
White visions tread the land
At your oblation
And everything that feels
Reels lightly in an unknown intoxication.

But you are a sublime messenger,
Freighting on the darker powers
Of a kindly force. And polarised
By your own receptivity,
You turn our outward face
Back to the greater face
We do not see: it sweats
A heavenly dew in magic
Numbers into the repose
Of lovers and the dance
Of the dead. Our stones
And our cities, our madmen
And geniuses, and the left-handed
Gate that leads to the regeneratory
Deep, we present
To your mysteries.
With you time quivers
And all our mortal illusions
Take on a new glamour.
You renew this landscape
That is our passing home,
You who lead us like a faithful
Guide in the dark,
Back to the transfigured
Gateway of the son,
Whose name is – beauty.

THE CRYSTALLINE QUARTZ,
OLDUVAI GORGE
2 MILLION YEARS AGO

Fire in the riverdream
And fear in the valley.
Night and the stone,
And hunger in the sky.
We carve these stones
With the sharp teeth
Of our dreams. Upright walk
The stone makers.

War calls in the distance.
On the move in the hills.
Rocks gush with water and lightning.
Night rises from the earth.
We sing songs to the wild heavens;
The gods listen to us in silence,
Then heave the earth with fire.

We lay down and breathe and cry out
The names that are secrets.
And then we make with stones
True items of our homes.
Our future, grainy as the sky,
Who can read it, save the gods?
And they are quiet now.

THE DIFFICULTY OF SEEING

It feels odd to look long
At a corpse or a leaf:
It disturbs one's belief.
I found it hard to see
My mother's face;
The more I looked,
The more her face eluded me.
I see her perfectly
In dreams, or when I don't try.
Then long afterwards
I wonder why I suddenly cry.

When you go to the seaside
At first you can't look at the sea
Or the horizon for too long.
Then, with time, it's like
Getting to know a strange song.
Whether it be faces, flowers, horizons
Something of the real
Is touched with a haze.
Reality resists the gaze.

ON KLEE

So you too were on the journey
To the East
Where mystery
Is the stuff of the feast.

Music and nature served you well.
Graceful and free, you wove your spell.
You find infinity in small spaces
And magic in the most likely places.

Not for you the noisy gesture,
The striking death or newsworthy posture.
Wisdom reigns in the hidden symmetry
And colours are but charmed invisibility.

What lingers in the soul
Often eludes the eye;
And the birds of heaven, without wings –
O how much more sublimely do they fly.

THE FIFTH CIRCLE

(After a reading of Dante)

1.

Anguish follows me down
These corridors. I see on the walls
Images of modern man fleeing
From the ravaging flies,
From border wars that never end,
From the gifts of life
Distorted in terror,
And from broken forms of power.
I wander, lost, in the satanic
Lights of the corridor.

The space opens. New images
Confront me, transfixing my gaze.
The corridor descends.
A light blazes downward.
The heat scalds me.
A mysterious presence
Wrenches me up.
My body slumps.
And I float out
Through the yellow ceiling.

2.

The fifth circle is closed.
Office hours are over.
A face with a melting
Cross in each eye
Stands before me.
The devil lifts me out
And places me here, with a grin.
A vulture nods at me,
And laughs.

Screams in the air sizzle my flesh.
History tramps on my nerves.
Skulls tumble at my feet,
Arguing about the principles of terror.
Then a hand from the sky
Lifts me into the dawn.
The kettle yells.
I catch myself
Becoming an idea.
The baby defeats history
With a howl.

CARPE DIEM: A LOVE SONG

I need someone to sing
To, can I sing to you?
My soul, a fountain, is bursting
With love that's strange and new.

I saw you standing there lovely
Like the roses of Spring.
I felt your mood soaring
Like bright birds on the wing.
And I heard your spirit's music of peace
Like the notes of the sea on coral reefs.

The beauty of your eyes
Speaks to me of the suffering
That youth weaves into love's offering
And then suddenly cries.

You love the world with all your youth
And all the rites of Spring and truth.
You love the world with your dreams too,
Your smile of sunlight, of diamonds blue.
You love the world with such a hard-won smile
With a heart that's free of guile
With a love of freedom, a joy immense,
And with the fire of a rare intelligence.

When I think of you my soul sings
Of rainbows and magic things.
Your voice rings in me like a golden bell.
You have the grace of an African gazelle.

The rich flow of your hair,
Your loving flair,
Your innocence of herbs that heal
Makes the god in me real.

You love the moon
And are kind to strangers:
And your serenity
Dissolves all dangers.

When my wounds are throbbing
And my soul with agony is ringing
Your sadness makes me dwell
Where the nightingales are singing.

Like light to bright mountains
I am drawn to your heart's fountains.
Your lightness and charged air
Make my being tremble, and my lips dare.

You are the mysterious smile
I never understood,
The surging dream,
The yellow mood.

Your gentle eyes alone
Redeem and bring much ease
To the sailor who must atone
And suffer the tumult of the seas.

The wounded warrior who's still bold
Needs your spirit's magical cure;
He's fighting for light far out in the cold
And he's still lonely and pure.

I have fought all life long.
I grow slowly and true.
Been growing slowly to be strong
For the day I meet you.

Even for pearls and gold
I would not queue
If I had the beautiful choice,
The simple choice, of loving you.

The flowers I can name
With all their poetic fame
Are names of nothing true
If they're not praising you.

Your silence heals the heart
Of the poet and the pilgrim of art
Who in the forge of time and dreams just might
Be touched with miracles of light.

You happy dawn, you radiant dove,
You make all things shimmer,
You make all things glimmer,
Because they shine with love.

I need someone to sing
To, can I sing to you?
My soul, a fountain, is bursting
With love that's strange and new.

THE POISONED ORACLE

Over the mighty bridges between
One world and another
Lie the grey mists
Of evaporating rivers,
Blue at night and
Yellow at dawn.

For the world is sizzling
In its own electronic heat.
Our ideas, generated
Whole from computers, turn
Human touch into myriad
Design, and stone:

For we no longer breathe
The air of dragons, or the winds
That propel lions to
Their granite caves

And the waters dry
Up with our touch
Because our love has for so long
Died during the longest winter
That has crept over the desert.

The birds no longer have to caw
And beat the air
With feathered wings.
They speak now with
Voices of stone.
Their wings are all of bone.

And we have sold our human flesh
And mighty tide of dreams
For tough indifference
And a brutal silence
In which we speak
And hear nothing but bones
    clicking
In our feathered throats.

MIGRATIONS

The world is a cauldron
In which we are mixed.
Time is an illusion.
No condition is fixed.

And so in our millions
We walk or swim or break
Across boundaries, fleeing
Wars, evils and hunger to make

A new home in what seems
A void, an empty space,
Without our histories,
Or tales of our race.

But about us scream the inhabitants
Who've never known barren
Lands, or tyranny, or such pain
That pushes us from the warren

Of cruel histories into lands
Whose earth may not receive
Us. But we're like pollen.
We're fertile, and we grieve.

THE AGE OF MAGIC

For Rosemary Clunie

Without knowing it we had crossed
A silver line in time. We had
Been in the dark age of iron.
It seemed to last forever.
And then one night the stars
Seemed brighter; a blue and orange
Fragrance of saffron floated in the air.
Children in the poor district saw,
At dawn, blinding flashes of a yellow
Angel's wings. That morning
There was a tingling feeling in our feet.

A mermaid with a piercing voice
Sang in the far reaches
Of the Thames. A beggar
Was seen levitating
At dusk on the outskirts of the city.

From the graveyard the skull
Of a dead poet recited
Forgotten *terza rimas* in reverse.
An alchemist on a barge turned
A dead pigeon into gold with
A black powder. But in the street
One afternoon a simple
Miracle took place when a woman laced
In reds and blues sprouted
Dark beautiful wings from behind
Her neck, under the astonished
Gaze of a gypsy child.
The age of iron is over.
The age of magic has begun.
Unveil your eyes.

NOSTALGIA

Like a ship in the sand
The days have moved slowly
But one never leaves land.
Dreams gather in black books:
Coiled spaces, mixed up parables
Out of which looks
The soul as it reads time.
I travel the whole world
With an uncomplicated rhyme.
I feast in dreams, and fast in life;
It seems that dreams transfigure strife.
So I send messages to my future
Within a murky paradigm.
Out at sea there are many rocks
I encounter before they are due;
Sleep resolves them in paradox.
Only in the present are things true.
Not even the future will last.
Nostalgia's a flower sent to the past.

VENUS AT HER TOILETTE

(After Velasquez)

Only the god of love may hold
The mirror in which you may look
(Without terror, without being bold)
Upon love's true nature, as in a book.

The eyes see but forms and the seven
Lonely colours. Not much heaven.
You may as well be blind.
All else majestic is seen in the mind.

These are my musings as I gaze
Upon myself, beyond all sight,
In the mirror in which, as in a haze,
Features are blurred with light.

I lie here in curves luminous.
All that you are lives in this place,
This magic casement numinous.
From your gaze I conceal my face

So that you may find me more real
In the mind's maze, and what hearts feel.
Unless it's to look within, with rigour,
Do not look too long into the mirror.

In there, within, you will find me:
The source of the mystery.

MODENA

For Contessa Fosco

1.

There's the music of birds
In the hedges.
Birds in the rain.
And there's the rain
Brought here in a bag from
The rain-cloud-ringed island.

Portraits in sun-touched skin
And a gold-covered green
And a face known for years
In silence, laughter, and in tears.

It's raining in the square
Where an old church
Quietly groans in *sfumato*.
Its accretions transport
A modest ardour in a stone
And pink fading
Mood. A square to dream in.

2.

But there is nothing left here.
Just the music and the sin
That is always forgiven,
The real sin of loving
And not speaking of it
To the one who should hear.

Speak but do not shout of love.
Speak it tenderly through the rain
And shelter it under the green.
That is what the music should mean.

ON THE OBLIQUE IN HORACE

We're not very good at looking
At life directly. Our eyes slide
From the full-frontal gaze
At the ordinary or the profound.
Direct things hide.

We are better at seeing life
Obliquely. From the corners
Of our minds. In the margins. On
The edge of vision. We
Are haunted by glimpses,
The barely seen.
We think about them more.

That's what true art is for:
To make us see what's important
Through a bending light.
(For truth dwells in mysterious night.)
By staying always oblique,
Always haunting, it lives
Longer in the mind of mankind:
Living longer for its mystery,
Its unfathomability.

And so beauty in poetry must *be:*
Being there and not being there.
Something at which you cannot stare
Something that hides in metaphors,
In paradox, or images,
Scenting the mind,
Fragile, yet enduring.
A death that's like a rose.
A birth that grows and grows.

The ancient masters, when they praise,
Seem to be doing something else.
But what they raise
Deepens the meaning
Much more than a direct
Song on the lyre.
Deepens it into the oblique
Places in you.
Places of divine fire
Where all the greatest things are known:
Hidden, eternal, true.

BASALT STONE, OLDUVAI GORGE
1.8 MILLION YEARS AGO

This is different. Three fires
In the dark. A world is coming alive;
And all the sky opens
To the coming of the god
With the fires all over the sky.

Who can weep now. The god
Has arrived, and power
Is furled into this shape.
Now, who knows, time has changed.
We hold the secret. Animals
Have heard us scratch
From the boiling
Rock this incantation
In stone. The will is now risen.
We can open the skulls.
We can beat music into bones.
We can heal by breaking.

We can break the secret
Of the sky in the valley.
We speak to the mountains
Of their hidden fire. We
Have become the mountain
With skyfire in our veins.

Maybe at night we join the gods.
And in the day, at dawn,
When the eagles scream, we become
Humans again, with wings
In our eyes, and fire in our hands
Turned to stone, to make twilight yield
Between gods and men a new time.
Dreaming is freed.

I SING A NEW FREEDOM

I sing a new freedom
In days of fire.
Freedom with discipline.
We need freedom to rise higher.
Be true to your true self
In the rich follies of our times.
Become the force you are
In this era of economic crimes.
Only those who remain free in spirit
Will find their way out of this maze.
But we are children of the stars,
And we ought to amaze.

AS CLOUDS DO DRIFT

1.

As clouds do drift above our heads
As dreams do flit above our beds
So time sieves through our lives.
Where does it go?
When it has passed
What do we have to show?

2.

We can plant deeds in time
As gardeners plant roses or thyme.
We can plant thoughts, or good words too
Especially if they are noble and true.
Time is an act of consciousness:
The source of fruitfulness.
To master it we are called;
It's one of the greatest forces
Of the material world.

3.

We ought to use time, like
Emperors of the mind;
Do magic things that the future,
Surprised, will find.

4.

We could transform our lives today,
Seek out a higher way.
The Buddha sat beneath a tree
And then from all illusions became free.
And as we travel this life that is a sea
We can have glimpses of eternity.

5.

We can join that growing fight
To stop our world being plunged into night.
We can wake to the power of our voice
Change the world with the power of our choice.
But there's nothing we can do
If we do not begin to think anew.
We're not much more than how we think;
In our minds we swim or sink.

6.

If there's one secret I'd like to share
It is that we are what we dream,
Or what we fear.
So dream a good dream today.
Keep it growing in every way.
Allow the moments of our life
To help us win the good fight
Or spread some light.

7.

The wise say life's a dream;
And soon the dream is done.
But what you did in the dreaming
Is all that counts beneath the sun.

8.

The dream is real,
And the real's a dream;
Each one of us
Is a powerful being.
Wake up to what you are,
Something of the sun, something of a star.
Wake up to what you can be.
Search, search for a high destiny.
While clouds do drift above our heads
And dreams do flit above our beds.

NEW YEAR POEM: O THAT ABSTRACT GARDEN

O that abstract garden of being
Tells me to be brave, and clear,
In the fire of living,
And in the journey through the year.
So I will grow me like an oak tree
And make life's honey like a bee.
Each day I will walk an interesting mile
And with the sun I'll share a smile.
I will play again like a child,
And celebrate what's wild.
I will swim in every sea or river,
And reflect the light of the sublime giver.
I will be at ease with opposition,
And will cultivate intuition.
I will walk the surprising streets,
And dance to life's unexpected beats.
I will notice all the phases of the moon
And try not to act too late or too soon.
I will write something new every day
And look at paintings in an alternative way.
I'll not dream the same way twice;
But I'll not be shy to repeat what's nice.
I'll have the courage, when needed, to change;
And I won't forget that life is strange.
And so I'll learn to love the simple things
As well as the complexity that life brings.

Good or bad I'll learn to treat the same
And I'll not forget that it's all a mysterious game.
I'll not let that general fear of death run my life
And I'll make magic even out of strife.
Into the higher realms I will enter
And make my corner the centre.
O that abstract garden, make me clear,
Make me brave, without fear.
I intend to love this rich new year.

A VISION OF TI
(At Saqqara, Egypt)

For Sven Johansson

I am beyond your reach,
Yet I am just next door.
I am in the next room,
Yet I am realms away.
I stand here in the other room
And no doors connect us.
You are sealed off from me;
And there is a rectangular gap
In the wall through which
You can see me.
I stand here, in eternity,
In the next room, gazed on
Now and then, through
A peep-hole.
I stand here like a god.
I am the image of the other world.
I am a man, in the magic
Age of forty,
Age of eternity.
And I am strong.
I am tranquil.
I have no fear.
I have gone beyond death.
I have survived the twelve
Gates; my heart has been weighed
On the scales, and is lighter
Than a feather.

I have not been devoured
By the crocodile
Or the many-headed monster
That gobbles hearts weighed down
With life's evils.
I have found my way back
To my body;
I am re-united in eternity.
I stand here, in this immortal
Space that you call a room,
And I stare straight at you
With a clear heart.
Will you survive
The monsters of the gate?
Will you come through
The fires of a life
And carry in your hand
The beauty of the lotus?
Do you have the simplicity
That the gods crown with grace?

I have wrestled
With the demons of the dark,
And been guided
By the angels of the light.
I have seen the glow of Orion.
I have bathed in the radiance of Sirius.
All the pyramids in me
Are aligned to the magic stars.
All the pharaohs in me are
In tune with the shining constellations.

I have summoned
The double-headed axe.
I have banished the crocodile.
My veins are charged
With the flow of the Nile.
My dreams are rich
With inundations
And the silt season.
Prosperity and true power
Will flourish from
The freshness of the land.
I have planted my future
In my past, and now its seeds
Reveal their growth
In your astonishment.
Do you see the power
Of pylons in my eyes?
When you gaze upon me
From that other room where
The living journey towards death,
When you gaze upon me
Through that hole in the wall
Don't you notice
The energy of the gods
Shining through me?
I am in the next door realm,
And your future is clear to me
As the desert is clear
To the sky.

Remember me, you who gaze
From the room
Of darkened lights;
Remember me, for I
Am that which lives
In that which dies.
I am the eyes
Of the mysteries.

HERACLITUS' GOLDEN RIVER

1.

'Change is good, but no change
Is better.' The words rang
Through the great hall
As they have resounded
Silently through bygone ages.

The air is dryer where no change
Is better. Old ways kept
Old, protected from the devils
At the gate, stiffen
The mind's luminous dance.
Change is a god that Heraclitus saw
In the ancient river.

And as we keep
Things the same, the river
Works beneath us,
The god works ironies
On our lives. The river runs;
Fields unfurl strange
New mushrooms; libraries yield
New books in the charged
Margins of the old.
And reason, trapped in iron philosophies,
Turns on itself, and prowls
The diminished boundaries
Of a shrinking world,
Shrinking because of the horror
Of the devils at the gates.

Poets pray to the goddess of surprise:
Love is seduced by change,
Itself unchanging. Time,
Serene, remains indifferent
To our iron will, our willed philosophies.
The world grows or shrinks of its own
Necessity, its own vision.
The river makes all things
Dance to a music they
Never understood at the time.

2.

The giants who built walls
Meant to be proof against
Time and the desert ravages
Found in their sleep
That the walls had become
Change, had moved, had dissolved;
Or worse, that the feared things
Had seeped in underfoot,
Or through the air;
Or changed the frontiers
Of their rigid dialogue.

Walls invite invasion.
Walls end up trapping within the demons
Meant to be kept out; for
The demons merely turn into
The giants, grow in them,
Like a silent cancer.

Oases attract the eyes of the hungry.
Protected places, illuminated
By fame, attract the rage
Of the unlucky, the unfortunate,
The dispossessed, and all those
Shut out in the outer
Darknesses of our age.

All around, leonids, planets,
Stars are whirling.
The cosmos shrinks and grows,
It dreams and flows
Beneath the immutable spell of change.
All around lives collapse, empires
Quietly fall and cave in from
Natural exhaustion; dynasties
Give up the ghost of ambition,
Continents drift apart,
And wars eat up fathers and frail sisters,
And roads break out
Into unhallowed speech.

It is natural to want calm places
Where stillness grows,
It's natural to want
Virgil's spreading beeches.

But the river flows, and so must we.
Change is the happy god Heraclitus
Glimpsed in the golden river.
Spread illumination through this darkening world,
Spread illumination through this darkening world.
No change is good; dancing
Gracefully with change is better.

O LION, ROAM NO MORE

(On the Death of my Father)

O father Lion roaming in my being,
(Our fathers are not what they seem)
Merge into me
Help me be free
Multiply my powers
Beyond the ancestral towers
Bless me with your wisdom
Guide me to my kingdom
Be the invisible warrior
In my life's upward fight
As I strive for more love
And for more light.

Do not be angry with your son,
Through him good battles will be won.
Don't fret about the years
When we couldn't speak.
Forget our mutual tears
There will be joy at life's true peak.

So do not fret, O Lion of the mind.
There is much to do for mankind.
Lend me your might
In the glorious fight
Lend me power
In the need of the hour
Send me radiance,
Majesty and fire

That I may grow stronger,
And climb higher.
Into my blood
Plant the secrets of the way
That I may live
More wisely every day.
Imbue me with your myth,
Solid silvery one,
That I be attuned
With the magic of the sun.

O Lion, rage and roam no more
In your son's troubled mind.
Rest now on that blessed shore
Where eternal light is most kind.